MODERATION

Kevin Kautzman

BROADWAY PLAY PUBLISHING INC
New York
www.broadwayplaypublishing.com
info@broadwayplaypublishing.com

Cover art: US Air Force photo illustration by Staff Sgt Jamal D Sutter. The appearance of US Department of Defense (DoD) visual information does not imply or constitute DoD endorsement.

First edition: December 2024
I S B N: 979-8-88856-043-3

Book design: Marie Donovan
Page make-up: Adobe InDesign
Typeface: Palatino

MODERATION received readings from 2020-2024 at the Blank, Broad Horizons, Spooky Action, and Up theatres and the Valdez Theatre Conference. An audio production of the Spooky Action reading was adapted by Crying Hill Media, for online release.

MODERATION was premiered by Bad Mouth Theatre Company at the Hive in Saint Paul, Minnesota, in October 2024. The cast and creative contributors were:

SHE .... Amanda Forstrom
HE ....Matthew Saxe

Co-direction ...... Kevin Kautzman & Meghan Gunderson
Sound design.. Ryan Condon
Stage manager...Maren Findlay
Video design...Abbie Lucas
Original music...Shawn Phillips
Lighting design .... Ariel Pinkerton
Graphic design .... Alex Forstrom
Production assistance .... Matthew Kelly
PR & social media...Mari Sitner

The UK premiere of MODERATION will be at the Hope Theatre, opening 19 March 2025. The cast and creative contributors will be:

SHE ....Alice Victoria Winslow
HE ....Robbie Curran

Direction ....Lydia Parker
Production .... Suzette Coon
Video design ....Abbie Lucas
Lighting design ....Jack Hathaway
Sound design .... Ryan Condon
Original music ....Shawn Phillips
Stage management ....Nathan Friend

CHARACTERS & SETTING

She
He

A content moderation center run by the Contractor on behalf of the Company's ubiquitous social media Platform.

In the premiere, the set consisted of two desks, two rolling office chairs, and greyscale then photonegative projections on the upstage wall (and actors) during content moderation.

ACT ONE: SEVEN PLUS, *morning*

ACT TWO: BIGFOOT & MUSSOLINI, *noon a month later*

ACT THREE: KILLDOZER, *afternoon a month later*

A note on the script:
— indicates an interruption
/ indicates overlapping speech

ACT ONE:
SEVEN PLUS

(Morning. Tapping at keyboards. Chirping of birds. SHE *and* HE *are at their computer terminals.)*

SHE: I am being a social media content moderator. He is being my manager.

HE: She is being my first direct report. Technically my second. The first one had issues. I am attempting to forget that loser. I am forgetting.

SHE: I am looking at video of Bigfoot. I am wondering why it was flagged. There is a male voice speaking, poorly recorded. And now I am understanding. The voice is claiming Bigfoot is a descendent of what the voice is calling "undesirable races". And I am snickering at how stupid this is despite myself.

HE: I am glancing at her. I am wondering what she is thinking is so amusing.

SHE: I am being seen by the one who is my manager. I am keeping a straight face. I am thinking this insane Bigfoot video would be hilarious if it did not have six thousand upvotes. I am flagging it for removal. I am looking at the next item in my queue. I am looking at this button in the corner of my screen. It is saying, "bio break". I am being tempted to tap it so I can go to the toilets and laugh about the Bigfoot racist. I am deciding not to, as it is my first day.

HE: I am looking at footage of the 9/11 attacks. I am watching a documentary about WTC Seven, the third tower in New York that went down that day. I am understanding why this was flagged, but I am uncertain whether this violates the terms of service. I am leaving it for now. I may look for it at home on my VPN. I am wondering how the Head of the Company would feel about this video, if he knows something we don't. I am wondering if he has government security clearance. I am realizing he has access to more information than the government. I am realizing the government probably asks him for clearance. Lucky bastard.

SHE: I am watching a video of Mussolini and his what, wife, girlfriend, mistress hang on meat hooks. I am hoping our break will come. I am moving my cursor nowhere, in a loop, nowhere in a loop…a loop…a loop…I am looping…

(*A soothing electronic sound ends their work session. The light of their monitors fades.*)

HE: That's our morning break. Twenty minutes. You catch anything very bad so far?

SHE: Some mild race baiting. We dodged the race war another day! Ha ha? I removed this stupid Bigfoot video but didn't suspend the account. I think they were trying to be humorous…

HE: Any sevens?

SHE: Threes and fours. Bigfoot was a six.

HE: If you get a seven plus, tap me.

SHE: Physically?

HE: You may tap me on the shoulder.

SHE: And may I have that in writing?

HE: That's not funny. Are you trying to be funny?

SHE: Yes.

HE: Let's just enjoy a nice quiet break, shall we?

SHE: Okay. I do have a question. Boss?

HE: Shoot.

SHE: How will I know if a piece of speech is a seven plus?

HE: Doxxing. Threats of violence. It's in the handbook.

SHE: What if they're joking? How will I know?

HE: How does anyone know anything?

SHE: What if I mistake a joke for something serious?

HE: Jokes make you L O L.

SHE: Not always.

HE: This is art, not science. The algorithm will flag anything suspicious—

SHE: Answer my question.

(HE *holds up his hand. The birds chirp.*)

HE: Don't interrupt me. Never interrupted me.

SHE: Sorry.

HE: If you get a school shooting or a beheading, you know what to do.

SHE: Remove.

HE: Suspend.

SHE: Report. Off with their heads.

HE: Yes. But speech is tricky.

SHE: In a way I'd prefer to see beheadings all day.

HE: You wouldn't.

SHE: Right. No.

HE: This isn't the French Revolution. Yet.

SHE: That's witty. "Yet."

HE: I'm renowned for my wit. On the Platform.

SHE: Do you have many friends? On the Platform.

HE: I do. And they all have heads attached to their bodies in their happy Platform headshots.

SHE: It would make the job easier. You see a video like that, you remove it and suspend the account. I could do that all day and not have to think.

HE: You'd have to be brainsick to think that.

SHE: Brainsick?

HE: The counselor is on the top floor.

SHE: Do you see them?

HE: I went once. I saw a thing with goldfishes.

SHE: Goldfish?

HE: Goldfishes. Two.

SHE: What did they do to the goldfishes?!

HE: I'd rather not say. The suicide livestreams used to freak me out. You get numb. Whatever happened to an old fashioned suicide note?

SHE: It's a dying form. Ha ha. Ha? Boss?

HE: People don't think about the strangers who have to watch this stuff. They could just leave a note for their loved ones. If they have any.

SHE: People use the technology at hand. So we go where tech directs. Even to the grave.

HE: Ahh, but tech goes where humans direct it. It's symbiotic.

SHE: Is it tho?

HE: "Humans are the sex organs of the machine world."

SHE: What? Gross. No.

HE: Yes. "Man becomes, as it were, the sex organs
of the machine world, as the bee of the plant world,
enabling it to fecundate and to evolve ever new
forms. The machine world reciprocates man's love
by expediting his wishes and desires, namely, in
providing him with wealth." McLuhan.

SHE: What if humans are the wealth of the machine
world? The machines desire content. We're content too.

HE: I'm malcontent. Ha ha. Pew pew. Finger guns.

SHE: You're malcontent content. Maybe that's what
the machines want. Maybe the future belongs to them,
and we just moderate the present for them til they take
over.

HE: But I have free will. I can choose to stop
moderating at any point. I'll demonstrate. I can choose
to ring this bell right here any time. Or not. (He holds
his hand over a bell on his desk.) Not ringing the bell. Still.
Choosing.

SHE: Tease.

HE withdraws his hand.

HE: I'll ring that bell when you make me L O L. Deal?

SHE: Deal. So I have another question. Boss?

HE: I'll allow it, since it's your first day.

SHE: What's the craziest thing you've seen in this job?

HE: Beyond the goldfishes?

SHE: What did they do to the goldfish?!

HE: Don't ask questions you don't want the answers to.

SHE: Poor fish. Fishes?

HE: Forget it.

SHE: What else?

HE: There was a thing with a child.

The birds chirp.

HE: People are monsters.
Then there are the conspiracy theories. I saw one yesterday that said: aliens bred with Neanderthals and that's how we got humans. And that relates to the fact currency isn't real and we're slaves with smartphones that owe money to some shadow power and nobody can say exactly who except it's Jews every time if you click the third link.

SHE: Jews. Classic.

HE: Sometimes the aliens and Jews work together.

SHE: And that's why you never read the comment section.

HE: Or click the third link.

SHE: Real. That's funny.

HE: It's not tho. People believe this stuff. And not just the Jew alien thing. Have you heard of the Killdozer?

SHE: The kill-what-now?

HE: The Killdozer. After the local council screwed with his business through zoning or something, a man in Colorado welded himself into a tank he made out of a bulldozer and destroyed a government building and a bunch of other stuff. When his "Killdozer" got stuck, he blew his brains out. Nobody else got hurt. There's a day where people celebrate this guy. Killdozer Day.

SHE: Why?

HE: Because he had enough and did something about it! You've never wanted to do something like that?

SHE: Bulldoze a government building?

HE: Not even once?

SHE: I still don't see how we can avoid reporting a joke by mistake.

HE: Context. You know the difference between some idiot using the n-word, like "Hey, my ninja" and some racist saying, "F you, ninja!"

SHE: Ninja?

HE: Yeah, as in: this is a break, we should be chillaxing, my ninja! What? Oh please. You started it. I'm perfectly content to just sit here quietly on my break.

SHE: And chillax?

HE: Yes. Like this. See? You should try it.

(HE *and* SHE *chillax. The birds chirp.* HE *taps at a phone.*)

SHE: So the terminals shut down on breaks?

HE: Yes. And remember: we're measured on performance against time. Every keystroke and mouse jiggle.

SHE: Jiggle?

HE: And they know where your eyes are at all times.

SHE: What if I have to use the bathroom?

HE: Tap the "bio break" button.

SHE: They track how long we're in the toilets?!

HE: Of course.

SHE: What if I fall in?

HE: Fall in?

SHE: To the toilet. Like what if I need to take like a really sticky dump/

HE: Whoa whoa whoa T M I.

SHE: I don't get the bell for that?

HE: I like a setup and a punchline.

SHE: Tough crowd.

HE: I'm old fashioned, I guess.

SHE: It's creepy, isn't it? The eye thing? Shit buttons?

HE: The Company knows what it's doing.

SHE: Why record eye movement?

HE: Consider the scale of this. There are tens of thousands of people doing this job/

SHE: Sure, but… Sorry. I interrupted.

HE: Thank you for catching yourself. I accept your apology.

SHE: Why track eye movement?

HE: This isn't chillaxing.

SHE: They're building a dataset to create a superintelligent AI. Qualitative reasoning. A conscious machine. Beyond the uncanny valley.

HE: Is that where we are?

SHE: How do we know this conscious machine isn't already here?

HE: The Company would demo it. Imagine the bump to the stock.

SHE: They'd field test it first. An embodied Turing Test. What's real, what's fake? Can a machine pass as human? But blind, with people who don't know they're subjects. They'll have signed away their rights in the terms of service.

HE: Nobody reads the terms of service.

SHE: Exactly.

HE: There is no way a secret superintelligence already exists. That would require a vast conspiracy. Kennedy on LSD. Hitler in Argentina. Kubrick and the moon landing.

SHE: What about the moon landing?

HE: Forget it.

SHE: You don't think we landed on the moon!

HE: I did not say that.

SHE: I bet you think the Earth is flat too.

HE: The Earth is round. We landed on the moon. There is no superintelligent AI. Yet.

SHE: Aha but what if they made the AI think it's human? Maybe that's the next phase of evolution. Machines that feel. A machine that's able to tell a suicide from an interpretive dance about suicide. Art appreciation.

HE: Machines will never appreciate art.

SHE: Sure they will. They'll know a mistake from a masterpiece, a finger-painting from a Pollock.

(HE *L O Ls a bit too loudly.* SHE *points to the bell.* HE *holds his hand over it.)*

SHE: That didn't have a setup or a punchline.

HE: Funny is funny. "A fingerpainting from a Pollock" is funny. To me.

SHE: Ring CLAP the CLAP bell CLAP.

HE: Wait did you do the clap emoji thing I R L?

SHE: Yes CLAP I CLAP DID CLAP.

HE: Why are you saying CLAP when you're clapping?

SHE: For emphasis. Ring the bell.

HE: I will. But, and please note this: I choose to ring the bell. Free will.

SHE: That doesn't prove you're human. You could be the first machine superintelligence for all we know.

HE: Wrong. They'll make it look like a woman. Hashtag fact.

SHE: Hashtag speculation. WAIT. What if they put two AI together and let them test each other? Turing squared.

HE: Way too dangerous.

SHE: Ring the bell.

HE: Even tho I laughed involuntarily a moment ago, I choose to ring this bell now. Free CLAP will CLAP… (*He rings the bell.*)

SHE: That's nice. Where'd you get the bell?

HE: I used to work front desk at a hotel. I took it on my last day back when I was a bad boy. Now I go by the books. Not much choice, is there?

SHE: Too many cameras. Too many rules.

HE: Speaking of rules. We get two twenty minute breaks, and a thirty minute lunch. Don't leave the building. Another twenty minute break after lunch. Do what you want on breaks. Quietly.

SHE: That's so boring.

HE: What would you rather do?

SHE: Well we could take a romantic walk to the restrooms together. Really dig into each other's "gender identity". Ha ha? No?

HE: Are you trying to flirt with me?

SHE: I'm trying to make you laugh!

HE: Sexual innuendo is not cool.

SHE: All right, Boss.

HE: I'm serious. The handbook explicitly forbids it, and for good reason. Things escalate very quickly when sex is involved.

SHE: I said "gender" not sex.

HE: I know what you said. I could write you up for it.

SHE: But you won't. Not today.

HE: How do you know that?

SHE: You recommended they hire me.

HE: Yes. So?

SHE: So it would reflect poorly on you to write me up on my first day.

HE: You could be reading a book right now.

SHE: I didn't bring one.

HE: So enjoy five minutes alone with your thoughts.

HE uses his device. Tap tap. The birds chirp.

SHE: What are you doing?

HE: Writing a screenplay.

SHE: Why can you have a device and I can't?

HE: After you pass probation, during breaks and in common areas such as the gender inclusive toilets, we are allowed personal electronic devices. This is to protect users' "right to privacy"—whatever that is. The first time they catch you with a personal device during a work session, you're fired. Read the handbook.

SHE: Did you read it?

HE: Three times. That's why I'm on management track.

SHE: Okay what's the screenplay about? Give me your pitch.

HE: It's about a dystopia in which an AI monitors everything and an elite group of managers run the AI and thus control the world. There's a great war between super-elite content moderators: Americans, Iranians, Israelis, Brits, Russians, the Chinese of course and a rogue outfit in Costa Rica. Germany has been returned to a state of feudalism.

SHE: Feudalism?

HE: In the Great War of the Prequels! And one of
the groups (*I won't say which, but wink wink it's the
Russians, because it's always the Russians when it's not
the Jewish lizard alien coalition*) controls the market on
dickpics with an algorithm that knows a dick when it
sees it, while the heroic Americans have to deal with
racist squirrel avatars using the word "nuts" as an
antisemitic dog whistle. It's called Dicks and Nuts.

SHE: You're messing with me.

HE: Nope. I already have the title for the sequel. "Dicks
and Nuts Two: Erection Night."

SHE: How are you not violating the handbook with
comments like this?

HE: What are you gonna do, report me?

SHE: No, of course not.

HE: There you go. We're gonna get along fine.

SHE: What's it really about?

HE: It's a romantic comedy set in a sub-basement office.
He's a struggling social media content moderator.
She's new. Her first day. He has a past, a dark side and
maybe he's starting to become unhinged by the job.
He's hearing things. Like birds that aren't there. Or
maybe the birds aren't even real.

(*The birds chirp.*)

SHE: That's not romantic or comic.

HE: That's where the humor is. The awkwardness.
The fact he's losing his mind and falling in love at the
same time. It's a metaphor. You know what that word
means?

SHE: I'm not stupid.

HE: It ends in death. Also a metaphor.

SHE: Do you know what that word means?

HE: Death? Wait and see. It might end in a murder suicide. But comic. A lot of physical humor. They're not just sitting at their desks the whole time.

SHE: Let me read it.

HE: It's not ready. I'll invite you to the table read when it's ready/

SHE: I bet it's funny. Let's read a scene quick/

HE: I said it's not ready. Hey, no!

(SHE *reaches for his phone.* HE *jerks her arm.*)

SHE: Fine! Damn!! OW!!! Jeeze. Man. Don't be so sensitive.

HE: Are you okay?

SHE: No, yes, it's fine. I invaded your space.

HE: Bring a book tomorrow.

(The birds chirp.)

HE: Please don't report me. I need this bump to management.

SHE: Aren't you my manager?

HE: It's a trial. This has to go well. The last guy quit after his first day. I need you to make it past probation. One month to probation and then another month after that. Then it's my review and I get my bump. I need my bump. You can't tell the others, but I have a friend at the Company.

SHE: Wait what? Really?

HE: I told you. I have friends on the Platform.

SHE: You didn't mention they work for the Company.

HE: One of them does. He likes my content.

SHE: You make content?

HE: Yes. I have a channel "Dumb Dad Jokes."

SHE: You're kidding.

HE: I am not.

SHE: You're not a Dad. Are you?

HE: You gotta start somewhere. See it. Be it. Live it. Anyway there's a management job for me at the Company if I can show management experience. What's good for me could be good for you. When I move up, you'll have a friend at the Company: me.

SHE: Wow…okay. Okay.

HE: You just need to make it a few months.

SHE: I'll try.

HE: It helps to know your "why." Why are you here really?

SHE: I want to be tech. In tech.

HE: Nobody is in tech to be in tech.

SHE: Honestly my "why" is my mother. She isn't well and I need to take care of her.

HE: Way too personal. I wouldn't mention that in an interview.

SHE: It's true tho. What's your "why?"

HE: I want to connect the world.

SHE: I don't believe you.

HE: This is distracting. I'm just trying to write one great line here, in my screenplay.

SHE: What's it about?

HE: What love is.

SHE: Love is a loaded gun.

HE: "Love is a loaded gun." That could work.

SHE: Nah, it's garbage. Let me think… Love is the zero and the one. Love is the birds chirping for what, for what reason, for love of something even tho we're in a deep basement and there shouldn't be birds chirping. Love is moderation. No. Love is excess. Wait, that's it. It's both, which means: love is a perfect joke, and the joke's on you. But you don't mind. That's what love is.

(*A gentle digital sound calls them back to work.*)

HE: I like "love is a loaded gun."

SHE: Don't go with the first thing that pops into your head.

HE: It wasn't my head. You want a drink? (*He reveals a flask from his on-brand tech bro satchel.*)

SHE: Sure? Thanks. Wow. Oof. Whew. What is that?

HE: Cajun vodka. Keeps me loose. Whoa there. That stuff ain't cheap.

SHE: Right. I'm worried about what I'm going to see this session.

HE: You'll be fine.

SHE: Can I ring it once for luck?

HE: I'd have to make you L O L first. That's the rule.

SHE: I need to ring it. It's driving me crazy.

HE: Do you like Dumb Dad Jokes?

SHE: Sure?

HE: Great. I heard this one on the Platform on International Dress Like a Pirate Day.

(SHE *holds her hand over the bell.*)

HE: So a pirate walks into a bar with a giant wheel on his crotch. He squats into a stool on the bar and the bartender looks at his parrot, then at the pirate's one good eye. The bartender slaps a shot of rum onto the bar and says, "Mr. Pirate. You know there's a giant wheel on your crotch?" To which the pirate replies: "ARRRRRRRGH. It's driving me nuts!"

(SHE *rings the bell.*)

SHE: Ha ha ha. Argh! It's driving me nuts.

HE: No no. AAAAAAAAAARGH! The key is the pirate sound.

SHE: AAAAAAAAARGH! It's driving me nuts!

HE: Back to work.

(HE *and* SHE *put on their headsets and glare at their monitors.*)

HE: I am looking at a series of images.

SHE: I am listening to an extreme political rant.

HE: I am scrolling through a series of images flagged for removal.

SHE: I am not believing this is my job, to see and report on these things, it doesn't seem real.

HE: The account has never posted anything suspicious, so I am moving on.

SHE: I am reading a political thread. Humans do not get along. I am wondering how anybody has this much time to waste on the Platform. But that is not my job.

HE: I am wondering how she is doing. She is being right there. I am worrying about what happened. I am wanting another drink. I am always wanting another drink.

SHE: There has to be a better way to make a living than this but I don't have any other options and I wanted to get into tech this is technically tech. Is it? It is a job and it is occurring to me I do not in fact know what love is. Love is not a loaded gun. Stupid. *(She flips her headset off slightly and turns to him.)* I can't believe this is a real job.

HE: Somebody has to do it. Stay focused. Get into a flow state. It goes faster.

SHE: I am staring at my monitor. I am doing nothing, which feels now like being nothing. I am being aware they are tracking my eye movement. I am in my own uncanny valley.

HE: I am looking at what appears to be a beheading from a year ago. Somewhere with sand. I've seen this one before…or have I? It is not mattering. It is a ten, and that is that. I am being thirsty. I am wondering if I am thirsty because I am looking at a desert. I am looking at blood. I am watching the video past what is necessary to file a report. I am watching the sinews and the bone come apart, and I am watching the head come off. *(He has another drink of the Cajun vodka.)*

SHE: I am considering the next brief. Something about a "developing situation" in London. And…this is a video with puppets so obviously a prank.

HE: People on their knees. A tourist or a journalist or both or you do not even know. It is the eyes that are the worst, in the head about to come off. They are begging with their eyes. Or they are crying for their mother, never their fathers. Why is that? I am watching this like you would watch paint drip to the ground. I am not feeling anything. I have seen it all. I am doing my job. Nothing
shocks
me

SHE: I am seeing something, a video. I am seeing something worse than. I am removing my headphones. I am standing back from the terminal. I am wondering how humanity is this broken. I am unable to look away. I am programmed to look. I am trained. *(She stands in shock.)*

HE: I am wondering this: you know how a beheading is going to end, so why post the whole thing? I am answering my own question, and the answer is fear. They want to remind us they exist because they feel forgotten. But so are we. Like the suicides. Same impulse. Same need. To be seen is to be remembered is to exist at all. Off with their heads.

SHE: I am covering my mouth with a hand. I am preparing to ring the bell with my other hand.

HE: Anyway it does not matter. A ten is a ten and I am flagging it and suspending. Some people do not deserve to live. I still do not know what love is. But maybe I am learning. I am glancing at my direct report. And it is being good to have someone here. I like her, yes. I decide I am liking her. She is making me less brainsick somehow. I am flagging the beheading account and what is she doing nobody told a joke…

(SHE *rings the bell.* HE *turns to her, headphones off.*)

HE: Nobody L O L'd.

SHE: I need to see the counselor.

HE: On your first day?

SHE: I'm sorry.

HE: Sorry? This is the job. If you don't like it, there's the door.

SHE: Please, just…I think…I can't.

(HE *stands from his desk and goes to hers. He taps at it. He stands back. He takes a drink. Another drink. He offers it to* SHE. *No)*

HE: I need you to not quit.

SHE: Boss. Is that real? Boss. Look at me.

HE: It could be a hoax. I'll need to do a deep dive.

SHE: I need a bio break.

HE: Escalate it to me, then tap the bio break button.

SHE: When I come back can that not be there?

HE: I'll take care of it. Look at me. You got unlucky. It's probably a hoax. Okay?

SHE: Okay.

HE: Thank you for the line.

SHE: What?

HE: "Love is a loaded gun." It's great.

SHE: It's garbage. A cliché.

HE: Please don't report me. For the thing, earlier. This job is my life. I am this job.

SHE: Thank you. For handling that. I need to ease into this. I already feel brainsick.

(The birds chirp.)

HE: Talk to the counselor. But please, come back. If not today, tomorrow. This is important work. The brainsick passes. You get used to it. The human mind can get used to anything. That's probably why we're so busy building our own replacements. We're too adaptable. Isn't that ironic? It got us here, and it'll be our downfall. That we can endure so much…

(SHE exits. HE goes to her terminal and looks. The birds chirp. HE finishes his Cajun vodka and leans over the terminal, staring. HE snaps to and goes to work.)

HE: Remove. Suspend. Report.
Off with their heads.

END OF ACT ONE

ACT TWO
BIGFOOT & MUSSOLINI

(Noon. HE *is alone at his terminal.)*

HE: I am flagging an account for doxing a journalist. This is an immediate suspension. I am making annotations. I am having a career in "tech." I am wondering if I am lying to myself. I am suppressing that thought. I am thinking about the next task. I am delaying slightly and looking at the "bio break" button but I don't need one and I have a sneaking suspicion they have sensors in the extremely inclusive toilets. I am wondering if I am being paranoid.
I am realizing what this is about is that I don't want to take a bio break right before lunch because it looks like I'm extending my lunch artificially and that would be a red flag. I am being hungry. I am looking at but not seeing the next brief. Another conspiracy video. World Trade Center Seven, the third building that came down in NYC on 9/11. Controlled demolition. "Pull it." The sky is falling. Eternal September. And it is almost time for…again, another one, not quite, almost and…there.

(A soothing sound signals lunch. SHE *appears.)*

HE: Don't take bio breaks right before lunch.

SHE: I'm a lady but I still take dumps.

HE: Ladies don't dump.

SHE: I'm a lady lumberjack. I dropped a giant log.

HE: Okay, can you just not/

SHE: Timberrrrrrr!

HE: Explain women to me.

SHE: Men are afraid women will L O L at them. Women are afraid men will kill them.

HE: Now explain ladies to me.

SHE: How much time do you have?

HE: Lunch just started. So thirty minutes.

SHE: It'll take an hour at least, and I'll have to charge you.

HE: Please tell me you brought a book.

SHE: I finished Mein Kampf last night. I'm onto the sequel but I forgot it at home.

HE: There's no sequel to Mein Kampf.

SHE: There is tho. It's a fan fiction thing on the darkweb, written in Spanish. Very weird. Very dark.

HE: I hope you're using a VPN.

SHE: It's called Su Lucha. YOUR Struggle. The goal is to finish the book before you blow your brains out. Total beach read.

HE: Yeah. Normandy.

(SHE *laughs.* HE *points. She rings the bell.*)

SHE: "Normandy." Nice. Pew pew. Finger guns.

(HE *taps at his mobile device again.*)

SHE: What are you doing? Hey! Boss! Put the device away. You can't stare at screens all day.

HE: Watch me.

SHE: You're gonna miss out then.

HE: On what?

SHE: I got you a present.

HE: For what?

SHE: My monthaversary.

SHE reveals a little electric moon lamp and figurine.

SHE: It's a moon lamp with a spaceman!

HE: Why?

SHE: So you can accept we landed on the moon.

HE: I never said we didn't land on the moon!

SHE: Let me turn it on. See? Don't let the conspiracies get to you, boss. It's not worth it.

HE: The moon landing footage was staged. That's all I meant. When you look at the stills and video you can't see stars. You can see flares from the lighting rigs. It doesn't make sense. It's clearly a sound stage. Look it up at home. I'm not kidding. Even the shadows look wrong. They come at crazy angles. You can see the wires in a bunch of the shots.

SHE: Wires?

HE: To fake low gravity! And they didn't include stars because astronomers would have done an analysis and called out their bullshit. It was a psyop. The greatest magic trick of all time. Maybe they landed on the thing, but certainly most if not all the footage was staged. You know NASA lost the telemetric data? For the missions to the moon?

SHE: No.

HE: Yes! So we're meant to believe we landed on the moon but don't have the mathematical records of the voyages.

SHE: You got all this from videos you flagged from removal?

HE: Yes?! So?!

SHE: We're supposed to report on this stuff and remove bad info, not get sucked down a rabbit hole.

HE: Yeah but once you see this stuff it's hard to go back.

SHE: I'm never going to believe in Bigfoot.

HE: No, but there's actual… Look up chemtrails. And fluoride. They're calcifying our pineal glands. Our third eyes. Fluoride lowers IQ! Fact!!

SHE: Okay, calm down.

HE: Fine, yeah. Thanks for the moon lamp.

SHE: Let's really see it in action. I'll get the light. *(She flips off the overhead lights.)*

SHE: So can we talk about the elephant in the room?

HE: Which?

SHE: My probation.

HE: Yes. Well I'm disappointed. Not in you. In the system.

SHE: "Performance concerns" they said?

HE: Yes.

SHE: My numbers are fine, right?

HE: You can't keep taking bio breaks right before lunch.

SHE: I could bring diapers and let rip like they do at the Company warehouses.

HE: This isn't a warehouse.

SHE: I can't control when I have to go. Why would I lie to get an extra five minutes?

HE: Maybe you're writing a screenplay. Turn the lights back on.

SHE: I started writing it after my first day I just didn't say because I wanted to get into the second act—

HE: I don't care. Don't give me your pitch. Please.

SHE: So here's my pitch: it's about a young woman who gets a low rung tech job because she has to support her sick mother.

HE: At least it's a rung! At least we don't live in a tent beneath an underpass! Turn the lights back on!

SHE: Her mother is dying from cancer. And they need to reconcile before she dies. You like it?

HE: I do not care CLAP Get the lights so I can finish lunch CLAP

SHE: You do it. I won't be spoken to that way.

(HE *stands. His shadow is long against the wall.*)

SHE: What? Boss. Are you okay?

HE: I don't like my shadow. Never did. Creeps me out.

(SHE *stands and turns on the light.*)

SHE: Okay. It's okay. Better?

HE: Yes. Thanks.

SHE: You want to talk about it? No?

HE: No.

SHE: Okay. How's your screenplay coming?

HE: It's not a screenplay. Never was. I'm next level.

SHE: What is it then?

HE: It's an interactive VR experience. More like an event that's also an interactive social media game on the Platform. Super meta.

SHE: Is this the one about the Russian squirrels or the romantic comedy?

HE: Both.

SHE: You're nuts.

HE: Nuts are squirrel currency. They went off the gold standard long ago, just like we did. You can look it up online, at home, on a VPN.

SHE: I don't have a VPN.

HE: Get one.

(*The birds chirp.* HE *pecks at his food.* SHE *leaves her desk and gets into a yoga routine.*)

HE: Where's your lunch?

SHE: I'm fasting.

HE: What? Why?

SHE: My body is a template. Temple. My body is a temple.

HE: It hurts me that you didn't pass probation. I told my contact at the Company you'd be thriving. Are you thriving?

SHE: Ask me after my fast.

HE: Have you tried leaning in?

SHE: Physically? Here. I'm leaning.

HE: Lean until you feel something.

SHE: I'm going to tip over.

HE: Now I can tell upper management that you're thriving since I taught you how to lean in.

SHE: Do they know my mother is ill?

HE: Is she really?

SHE: Isn't she? How would you know? How would the Company?

HE: They know everything.

SHE: How does anyone know anything?

HE: Touché.

SHE: You think they check that deeply?

HE: Their business is information. We volunteer it in order to "get connected," and they sell our lives back to us at a premium, with layers of algorithmic manipulation.

SHE: So?

HE: So we are the product. Of course they take inventory.

SHE: I'll make a post or two asking people to "pray for my family." Could mean anything. How's that?

HE: You'd lie for me? On the Platform?

SHE: My mother is actually sick. She just doesn't post about it. She's very private.

HE: Okay. Wink wink. Nudge.

SHE: I'll post something about it if you'll pray. Will you pray for my family?

(HE *L O Ls and L O Ls and rings his bell.*)

HE: Pray for your family…ha ha ha. Thoughts and prayers. Hashtag thoughts and prayers.

SHE: It's not that funny.

HE: You aren't hungry? Have a bite.

SHE: I'm fasting.

HE: I get it. Gotta exercise some discipline. I took a break from drinking a month ago. After your first day. It got out of hand. I might quit for good.

SHE: Good for you.

HE: I got a coin. Here.

SHE: You joined a support group?

HE: Oh no no no. I don't do I R L groups.

SHE: What about friends? Do you do I R L friends?

HE: My friends are on the Platform.

SHE: Where'd you get the coin then?

HE: I had it 3D printed. See on one side it says "congrats" and on the other it says "keep writing your experiential VR romantic comedy game, you're a massive winner, bro".

SHE: Wow. Yeah. I see that.

HE: So about your probation. I think it was the excessive bio breaks. And the psych visit, the first day before lunch. Massive red flag.

SHE: Did they consider what I had to see?

HE: They read my report.

SHE: Did they look at it themselves?

HE: We look so they don't have to.

SHE: They should have to. We're not machines.

HE: Prove it.

SHE: Enough of the AI bullshit!

HE: You started it! On your first day! Which is exactly what an AI would do!

SHE: What?! Why!?

HE: To trick me.

SHE: Be serious. We're talking about our careers here. We are not machines, and leadership should have to see what we do if they're going to pass judgement on us.

HE: It's our job to look at that stuff. They assess our performance. That's their job. That and the total dominance of the global population through harvesting personal information at scale.

SHE: That's cynical.

HE: It's realistic. Zoom out and consider what they achieved. They got people to self report to a central electronic system. How'd they get billions of people to do that?

SHE: The need to feel included.

HE: Fear. The Platform is built on fear. Fear of missing out. Fear of being forgotten.

SHE: Leadership should have to see the same dark shit we do if they're going to judge us for getting brainsick.

HE: Leadership isn't going to audit every extreme video we report. Imagine the impact on their productivity.

SHE: What do they produce?!

HE: These jobs! They have important meetings with the Company. They need to focus on the big picture. They have summits to attend. Conferences. Soft skills to master like, ahh, active listening. They have to smile on demand and make it look easy!

SHE: Watch me smile. I'm smiling. It's easy!

HE: You look like you want to tear out my throat.

SHE: How about now?

HE: Better. Now I believe you.

SHE: It's easy.

HE: You signed up for this. Our job is to moderate this shit so they don't have to. Division of labor. If you don't like it, there's the door.

SHE: Fine. You know what? I'd rather not have a half-assed performance review at lunch.

(The birds chirp. HE *eats.)*

SHE: Did you see the counselor?

HE: Too busy. I'm focused on the future and my award-winning VR game script.

SHE: You won an award?

HE: Not yet. Positive thinking. Ha ha. Finger guns. Pew pew. Leaning in. Pew pew. See it. Be it. Live it. I could start a coaching program and become a "thought leader." Tell people to smile more, backed by decades of pseudo-scientific research. You have to want it. You have to own your smile. Own it, be it, see it. OBS. Oh that's catchy. OBS.

SHE: What was the thing we saw on my first day? Was it a deepfake or/

HE: If I wanted to talk about it, I'd have brought it up by now!

SHE: Stop talking over me! I don't interrupt you!

HE: You're my subordinate! Do I need to get out the org chart?!

SHE: I want to talk about the thing we saw on my first day.

HE: You don't want a half-assed performance review over lunch. I don't want to talk about the thing we saw.

SHE: We're not paid enough.

HE: No shit. It feels…sometimes it feels like they're running an experiment on us. It's not about the money. It's about something bigger. Makes you want to do something drastic.

SHE: You sound like content we'd wipe from the Platform.

HE: You going to flag me for removal?

SHE: You know you can see the counselor any time, right?

HE: Of course. You know how I know? I read the handbook. Read the handbook!

SHE: She says I need to compartmentalize. Meditate. I've tried. My mind races. I haven't slept well lately. I have these dreams. I try melatonin but it doesn't help. Chamomile tea. I'm worried about what I might see next every time I complete a report. I'm worried about whether I'll make probation next month. It's hard to cope, and I think it's/

HE: It's not our job to think.

SHE: Well who's job is that?

HE: The Company! Upper management. The consultants with the Behavioral Psych PhDs and the speaking tours and the books. The Real People with the organic food and acupuncture and private coaching sessions.

SHE: And you want to join their ranks. Level up.

HE: I want security. I'm human.

SHE: Prove it.

HE: Are we back on that?

SHE: A male human being. Prove it.

HE: You want me to whip my dick out?!

SHE: Then I'd definitely have to report you.

HE: Wait did you file a report on me?! If you did, tell me. I can't get a bad review before the Company makes its calls over here.

SHE: I did not file a report.

HE: Did you tell anyone?

SHE: The counselor? That's confidential. It has to be confidential/

(HE *groans and slams the handbook once, twice, again.*)

HE: Read the handbook!!!

SHE: Calm down!

HE: It's my fault. I should have sat here and watched you read the handbook during a break instead of all this clever back and forth killing time bullshit.

SHE: I'm sorry, I'll read the handbook/

HE: Is this a game to you?!

SHE: What I tell the counselor is confidential.

HE: Unless she perceives a threat to safety.

SHE: You understand behavior like this is frightening.

HE: I get one shot to move up to the Company. They have a long memory. My record isn't spotless. I'm brainsick and it affects me sometimes.

SHE: I didn't report you.

HE: You didn't pass probation either. And you told the counselor about what happened.

SHE: My career doesn't exist to serve yours.

HE: But it could! Because mine could serve yours if you'd let it. We could have solidarity, instead of whatever this is.

SHE: So sit down and finish lunch. Sit! Eat your lunch. Come on.

(HE *sits at his desk.*)

HE: I lost my appetite.

SHE: Give me your lunch.

HE: Aren't you fasting?

SHE: Fear makes me hungry.

HE: I'm saving this for dinner.

SHE: You offered me some earlier.

HE: This is expensive. From the Company store.

SHE: Give me a bite.

HE feeds her a bite. The birds chirp.

SHE: This is what Company food tastes like?

HE: Only the best.

SHE: How do you get in?

HE: After you're here for a year, you're allowed to shop at the Company store twice a quarter. As per the handbook.

SHE: Give me another bite.

(HE *does.*)

HE: At the Company offices they provide food. Like this. They have everything you could want. Sushi. Actual fishes. And not farmed fishes. Fishes from the ocean. Indian food. Italian food. Coffee. Decaf coffee. Whatever you want. And you don't pay. It's part of comp. So you make fuck you money and don't even pay for lunch. They invented the free lunch.

SHE: Nothing's free.

HE: Sure it is. You just have to change how you see the arrangement. The Company rules the world. May as well be on their good side.

SHE: Tell me why you want to join the Company. Come on. Practice for your interview.

HE: I want to connect the world.

SHE: I don't believe you.

HE: I want to connect the world. I really do. How's that?

SHE: Say it with a smile.

HE: I want to connect the world.

SHE: Why? Why really?

HE: I never felt connected. Like with other humans.
People.

SHE: Oh. Well everyone feels that way sometimes.

HE: Not the way I feel…felt. That. That's why the
Company's mission is so great. Nobody should be left
out, left out of history or…like the flow of things. I felt
like an alien.

SHE: You're painfully normal. I'm sure you'll get the
position. See the counselor and get an interview coach.
And promise me you'll stop throwing shit fits, or I
really will have to report you.

HE: I apologize. I'm under a lot of pressure. My
brainsick is showing. But I'm not crazy. It's… you
know we can't be certain they're not running an
experiment on us? How could we know? It's like the
AI question. We couldn't know. I don't know. Are you
a machine? You don't even know. You can't.

SHE: This won't help my insomnia.

HE: Talk to the counselor.

SHE: I'm talking to you. I keep having this dream.

HE: Am I in it?

SHE: No…

HE: Then CLAP I CLAP don't CLAP care CLAP. (*He
reveals his phone and taps at it.*)

SHE: In my dream, I'm watching Bigfoot and he's very
lonely.

HE: Shut up. Nobody cares about somebody else's
dream if they're not in it.

SHE: He looks like…well he looks like you now I think
about it.

HE: Bigfoot looks like me?

SHE: Yeah… And Bigfoot, he's…strange, he just wants to fit in with us, with humanity. He wants to be one of us. He wants a "meaningful job." Because that's how you fit in. That's how you get along. He really is a lot like you actually. Afraid of his own shadow.
So at noon Bigfoot goes to the employment office, and the only job they have for him is in World War II. And there's Mussolini and his girlfriend or wife or mistress or whatever
And his body keeps falling off
the
hook
Somebody has to put it back. Some body has to do that so. That's a job for Bigfoot. And that's how the creature, that fantasy creature, finds his place.
He hoists Mussolini's corpse back onto the hook over and over, and when I wake up it feels like I haven't slept at all, because Bigfoot hasn't and can't and might never sleep again, not really, not the way you can when you know things are okay, and cared for, and the world is going to be all right, when you know you can always escape into the woods and maybe somebody will catch a quick glimpse of you but never the whole of you, that you'll never be reduced to a series of images, to somebody else's idea of you reduced to your digital echo, which isn't the real you at all.
A shadow reflected from something that's not even there.

(The birds chirp.)

SHE: You think they're tracking the birds too? Like the sound of the birds chirping?

HE: They say the government replaced birds with surveillance drones years ago. Try and prove they didn't. You can't. Like the AI thing.

(The birds chirp.)

SHE: Can we just talk like real people?

HE: Real people? What do real people discuss?

SHE: I don't know. Dreams?

HE: Dreams?

SHE: Sure. Tell me a dream you had.

HE: I don't dream.

SHE: Then tell me something real. Something you believe.

HE: I don't have beliefs. I only have disbeliefs

SHE: What do you disbelieve?

HE: I disbelieve the official 9/11 story.

SHE: Okay. Why?

HE: Ask most people how many buildings came down in New York City, they'll say two.

SHE: Isn't that right?

HE: Three.

SHE: Right, yeah.

HE: Sleight of hand. A trick. A media trick. Content moderation. WTC one, two, seven. Most people don't remember seven, or more precisely they don't know seven happened. There's no video of plane wreckage at the Pentagon. There's no video of a plane even approaching the Pentagon. These are just the obvious things.

SHE: So what'd they do with that plane? And the people?

HE: How much time do you have?

SHE: You do dream. This is a waking dream. A nightmare people on the Platform make real. A myth.

HE: Do your own research. At home. On your VPN.

SHE: We're meant to remove the conspiracy videos. And suspend the accounts. Right?

HE: Depends on context.

SHE: Give me the rest of your lunch.

HE: What? No.

SHE: So let me get this straight: some "shadow power" brought down WTC Seven?

HE: Maybe.

SHE: Who was it? The Russians? The Jewish alien coalition?

HE: I wouldn't rule anything out.

SHE: I wonder what management would think about that… Give it to me. I'm not asking again.

HE: Okay, you win. Eat your free lunch and shut your trap.

(SHE *eats, sniggering between bites.*)

HE: Don't L O L at me. Leave me some. I don't have anything at home.

SHE: Answer a question and maybe I'll save you a bite. I'm H R. Tell me why you want to work for the Company.

HE: I want to connect the world.

SHE: Don't just parrot our mission statement. Be real. You want the tasty food. You want the security. You want the status. Tell me the truth.

HE: The truth? Nobody should have to do this job as long as I have. I'm losing my goddamned mind.

SHE: Way too personal. I wouldn't mention that in an interview.

HE: Let's get through this and I'll help you come up to the Company once I have a foothold.

SHE: How long will that take?

HE: Maybe a year. Stop! That's all I have for dinner. Great. That's great. You're not a lady. You're a pig.

SHE: I'm a lady. Say it. Go on.

HE: Or what?

SHE: I'll report you for violent, threatening behavior. And sexual harassment. Say it.

HE: You're a lady.

SHE: Curtsy to me.

HE: Men don't curtsy. Men bow.

SHE: Curtsy or I report you.

HE: Don't be cruel.

SHE: This is no longer a safe space for me until I see you curtsy. Go ahead. Stand up. They told me what happened with the first guy you tried to manage. Now curtsy. Deeper. Lift your skirt. There you go.

HE: Who told you about the first guy?

SHE: They. The others.

HE: What did they say?

SHE: He didn't quit his first day. He made it a whole month. You lied. Why?

HE: I didn't want to freak you out.

SHE: Did he really bring a knife?

HE: More like a machete.

SHE: Why did he bring a machete to the office?

HE: There was a rumor somebody brought a gun and threatened a manager, at another office. Word got around. He got paranoid. This job isn't for everybody.

SHE: No shit. What do we do if there's an active shooter?

HE: For the final time: read the handbook.

SHE: Okay… What? Stop staring. You're creeping me out/

HE: You know I really did think you're an AI sent to test me. In bed, alone, late at night, wondering about my life and that day, your first day, what went wrong, where I messed up. I entertained the thought, that you're a machine and I'm a guinea pig in an experiment and you're my Turing Test. From the Company, vetting me for the position with them. You know?

SHE: See the counselor.

HE: I'm your boss. Don't forget that.

SHE: I need a bio break.

HE: Really? Lunch is almost over.

SHE: I'll be quick.

HE: Don't fall in.

(SHE *exits. The birds chirp. From his satchel* HE *reveals his phone and a handgun.*)

(HE *turns the phone on himself and records a livestream in such a way that the audience on the Platform cannot see the gun.*)

HE: Hey, guys and gal! Just livestreaming here on my lunch break. My subordinate is using the gender neutral toilets like she always does before breaks. She's a bit of a cheat but I think she really likes me. I think I've got a shot. A lot of sexual tension. If I can get promoted to the Company, I'll make enough money I can take her out and tell her she doesn't need a job anyway. I'll provide for both of us. Do it the right way. Tell her I want kids. I have to take it slow tho. Anyway I'm gonna give you your daily dose of dumb dad jokes. Are you ready? Did you hear about the restaurant on the moon? Great food, no atmosphere. Ha ha ha ha. What do you call a fake noodle? An impasta. I just watched a program about beavers. It was the best dam program I've ever seen! Okay thanks for watching. Smash that like button and share this channel if you like what I'm doing!

(HE *puts the gun back into his bag.* SHE *returns.)*

SHE: Did I make it?

HE: Barely.

SHE: Told you I'd be fast. So listen. The Company has a program for women.

HE: A program?

SHE: "Lady Tech Stars." It's a fast track to management at the Company. I've already got a spot and they haven't even announced the winner. Positive thinking! Finger guns. Pew pew. I told you I'm a lady.

HE: When's the deadline?

SHE: Yesterday.

HE: You applied?

SHE: Of course. Don't worry. It's very competitive.

HE: You could have told me.

SHE: And you could have told me about the program.

HE: I'm a man. It wasn't on my radar.

SHE: Well I'm a lady and I applied. I wrote a very strong essay. About my mother. She's very ill, you know.

HE: Bullshit! That is just bullshit! You're such a fake.

(A soothing electronic sound calls them back to work.)

SHE: If you throw another shitfit I'm gonna report you.

HE: Fine. But I know you're lying about your mother. If you get into the Company on some gynocratic DEI bullshit, I swear I'm going to lose my—

(SHE *reveals a mobile device.* HE *chases her around the desks.*)

HE: Hey! You can't use that! You didn't pass probation! The terminals are coming online! Come on, don't! You can't have that on right now! Put it away!

(SHE *shows* HE *the screen.*)

SHE: Look. My mother. There she is with her wig. There she is without it. Chemo is a bitch.

HE: Put it away. Please.

(SHE *puts the device away.*)

HE: Let's just get through the afternoon. No more games?

SHE: What games?

(HE *and* SHE *put their headsets on and turn to their illuminated monitors.*)

SHE: I am watching a young uhh white male enter a mosque and oh I have heard this joke before. A white supremacist, a Rabbi, and an Imam enter a mosque. There is no punchline. It is just gunfire BANG BANG BANG and death ugh ah oh please help and it plays on an endless loop suspend remove report report off with their heads.

HE: I am observing a shadow. I can't do this I can not do this job, not when I am this brainsick and she is fuck me I think I am maybe in love with her now and I do not know why I am am not, I am that I am not that I am my shadow and…

(SHE *turns to* HE *and removes her headphones.*)

SHE: Hey? Are you okay?

HE: I am. I am not. I am that I am not. My shadow is, that I am not. And so I cannot be, not really. Not real. Argh, it's driving me nuts. Ha ha. Aaaaaargh.

SHE: Hey. Take a bio break if you need.

(HE *rings the bell once, twice, again.*)

SHE: Are you okay?

HE: You know I could report you for harassment too? Then you'd never be a Lady Tech Star.

SHE: Please don't.

HE: You ate my lunch and made me curtsy.

SHE: It was a joke. I thought we were having fun.

HE: Fun?

SHE: Yeah. Killing time?

(HE *puts his headset on and turns to his monitor.*)

SHE: Finger guns. Pew pew? Pew?

HE: Shut up and do your job.

END OF ACT TWO

ACT THREE:
KILLDOZER

(Afternoon. HE *and* SHE *are at their terminals. On her desk is a fishbowl with two goldfish[es].)*

SHE: I am watching a video of a bulldozer destroy a building. Oh, I am realizing this is the Killdozer he told me about. It is Killdozer Day. These people are being crazy. Killdozer Day. But I am being unable to look away.

HE: I am listening to a voice. It is saying…

SHE: Project MKUltra is the code name given to a program of experiments on human subjects that were designed and undertaken by the Central Intelligence Agency and which were, at times, illegal.

HE: The Industrial Revolution and its consequences have been a disaster for the human race.

SHE: Experiments on humans were intended to identify and develop drugs and procedures to be used in interrogations in order to weaken the individual and force confessions through mind control. And I am listening to a voice. It is saying…

HE: The continued development of technology will worsen the situation. It will certainly subject human being to greater indignities and inflict greater damage on the natural world, it will probably lead to greater social disruption and psychological suffering.

SHE: I am unsure what to do with this video.

(SHE *removes her headphones, reaches over and taps* HE's *shoulder. He removes his headphones.*)

SHE: I got a Killdozer video.

HE: It's Killdozer Day. They're pretty much harmless.

SHE: This one has a voiceover. Listen.

(SHE *puts her headset on* HE's *head.*)

HE: Ahh yeah. He's reading Uncle Ted. Kaczynski? The Unabomber. Yeah, I take it back. This is a white separatist account. I've heard this guy a thousand times.

SHE: Okay, but it's still just speech. And Uncle Ted wasn't wrong, was he?

HE: Right or wrong doesn't matter. It's about context. He's reading this over video of a guy bulldozing a government building. And this is a racist organization dedicated to the overthrow of "ZOG". Use your eyes. It's a giant dog whistle. The dogs are freaking out.

SHE: ZOG?

HE: Zionist Occupied Government. There are Nazis are all over the Platform. You kill one of their accounts, another pops up. It's a game of whack-a-fascist.

SHE: Okay, well. Remove. Suspend. Report.

HE & SHE: Off with their heads.

(*A soothing electronic sound signals a break.*)

SHE: Last break on Friday. Home stretch.

HE: Yep. Oh, check it out. (*He reaches into his bag and reveals a cupcake and a bottle of wine with a screw cap top.*) It's a cupcake from the Company store. And wine, and plastic cups.

SHE: You're drinking again?

HE: In moderation. We're celebrating!

SHE: What are we celebrating?

HE: You made probation!

SHE: Amazing. Thanks.

HE: You can use a personal electronic device on breaks starting next week!

SHE: Yay personal electronic devices!

HE: Upper management will tell you on Monday. Just act surprised.

SHE: I can do that.

(HE *pours wine.*)

HE: A toast to the newly minted, official Junior Content Moderator.

SHE: This is too much.

HE turns out the lights.

SHE: Why'd you turn out the lights?

HE: To set a mood. Damn, I forgot the candle. We can pretend. Pretend there's a candle.

SHE: Aren't you scared of your shadow anymore?

HE: Nope. I saw the counselor four times this past month. And I've been meditating. The government spy birds don't even bother me so much anymore. And I'm pretty sure the Earth is round after all.

SHE: You're funny.

HE: Plus I'm heading toward my shot with the Company. I want to put my best foot forward, and that means self care and taking mental health seriously. Make a wish.

SHE: It's not my birthday.

HE: There's a candle. See? So you have to make a wish.

(SHE *blows out the imaginary candle.*)

HE: What'd you wish for?

SHE: It's bad luck to say.

HE: True. So how's your mother?

SHE: Better. Can we turn the lights back on?

HE: Oh, a miraculous recovery? I'm so glad.

SHE: Turn the light on. Now. Please.

(HE *does.*)

HE: Better?

SHE: Yes. This is sweet of you/

HE: I'm a sweetheart. Here. More wine? Only the best for my number one and only direct report. What are you doing this weekend?

SHE: No plans. Why?

HE: Just asking.

SHE: So, ah, what are you doing this weekend?

HE: Working on my stage play.

SHE: Your what?

HE: The VR screenplay game concept is a stage play now. It was a stage play all along.

SHE: Like live theatre?

HE: Yes.

SHE: Gross.

HE: No, it's great. The ancient hologram. Highly ironic. A metaphor.

SHE: Is there money in stage plays?

HE: It's not about the money. It's about status. Fame. Parties.

SHE: What about personal expression? Telling the story only you can tell?

HE: Whatever. Wow. That's hilarious.

SHE: So what? Is it the same idea? With the Russian squirrels?

HE: No. It's the romantic comedy about content moderators who might be falling in love while they lose their minds at work. You get it?

SHE: Not really.

HE: Because that's what love does. Love drives you crazy.

SHE: I guess.

HE: Yeah so they're falling in love and losing their minds at the same time, because of all the shit they have to deal with and how unjust and horrifying the world has become and they're a part of it and finally impotent to change anything but get this… I bet you can't guess what finally saves them.

SHE: Please tell me it isn't… It's not love, is it?

(HE *rings the bell.*)

HE: It's love!

SHE: Wow. Yeah. Love.

HE: So do you like it? My idea?

SHE: It needs a better ending.

HE: You don't think love saves them?

SHE: No.

HE: Why not?

SHE: Nobody will believe it.

HE: You're wrong. People love workplace romance. She's his direct report, and he's a little rough…a little on edge. You know? Brainsick but cute. And despite that he makes a series of romantic gestures, gets called up to the Big League at the Company, and she realizes how much she misses him after he's gone. It's called "Love is a Loaded Gun". What do you think?

SHE: I think you're brainsick.

HE: The title's a bit trash. You're not getting a credit, so don't ask.
It's cliché but catchy. You need something that grabs people and says, "Hey, come and see my stage play and invite me to an amazing party afterward where there's organic food and wine the people speak in complete sentences until they pair off and form these incredible I R L relationships." And nobody brings out a device, for one evening. And we are free from the tech overlords again, if only for a moment.

SHE: Parties are nice.

HE: I'm reaching for the stars. Pew pew. I'm gonna shoot the stars from the sky and stage another moon landing. Pew pew. Finger guns. I might take a shot at some Lady Tech Stars too, if they get out of line.

SHE: That's not funny.

HE: It's a metaphor.

SHE: I don't think you know what that word means.

HE: Sure I do. It's when one thing stands in for something else. When something takes something else's place.

(There is a soothing electronic sound, and his terminal comes back on.)

SHE: It's more than… Hey. Your monitor is back online. Break's not over, is it?

HE: No. Oh. Weird. They want to see me upstairs.

SHE: Important management business?

HE: Doesn't say. *(He screws the cap back on the wine and returns it to his satchel.)* This is the good stuff. Gonna save some for later. How was the cupcake?

SHE: Very good. Thanks. You're a good boss, boss.

HE: I'll be back soon.

(He exits, leaving his bag. She drinks her wine.)

SHE: Ugh. Stage play. He's insane. Brainsick. *(She rings the bell. She finishes her wine. She swirls the glass. She digs into his satchel and reveals the wine bottle. She helps herself to some of it.)* The Industrial Revolution and its consequences have been a disaster for the human race. *(She returns the wine bottle to the satchel, freezes, stares. She stands back. She leans. She pulls the handgun from the bag.)* Oh. Whoa boy. Whoa. Whoa doggy. Whoa mama. Whoa whoa whoa.

(She sets the gun into the bag and returns the wine. She chugs her wine and rushes to tap at her phone. He returns.)

HE: When were you going to tell me?

SHE: Tell you what?

HE: Put the device away.
You got into the program. When were you going to tell me?

SHE: I found out yesterday. It starts in two weeks.

HE: You're gonna be a "Lady Tech Star"?

SHE: I'm already a "Lady Tech Star". It's a mentality. I'm leaning in, like you taught me. Own it, be it, see it. I'm doing what's best for my career. There was an opportunity, I went for it. Self interest. Human.

HE: You mentioned your mother, in your application essay?

SHE: Of course. They want stories like that. People love to pity. Anything to feel superior. They'll give you the world if you bow to them at the right time.

HE: I don't bow. I curtsy.

SHE: You need to relax. Talk to the—

HE: Did you stage that photo? With your mother and the chemo and the wig? Like they staged the moon landing?

SHE: That question is totally inappropriate.

HE: When did you report me?

SHE: I never reported you. Formally.

HE: I need more wine. *(He pulls the bottle from his bag.)* You drank some of my wine, you sneak. Just like you ate my lunch. Just like you reported me behind my back. I'm not stupid. Doesn't matter. I'm off management track. They're putting me back in rotation up on three.

SHE: I'm sorry.

HE: I definitely need to finish my stage play now.

SHE: That's a good idea.

HE: Your leaving hurts me very badly. You and your bullshit program.

SHE: That's not true. You made a good hire. It just didn't work out.

HE: You're leaving. You're the second direct report they gave me. The first one brought a machete. Now you're leaving after two months.

SHE: It's just bad luck.

HE: I'm cursed. Or they're experimenting on me. Both. I get it now. I'm not Bigfoot. I'm a goldfish. *(He pours wine into the goldfish bowl.)*

SHE: See that's a…metaphor.

HE: No, I'm literally a goldfish.

(*The birds chirp.*)

SHE: You're paranoid.

HE: I'm not tho. They're running an experiment on me, and you're in on it.

SHE: It's only an experiment in the sense that…this digital world, with all this tech, well everyone's a part of the giant lab they're running…

HE: It's inhuman.

SHE: What you feel is normal. The Platform is social engineering on a scale beyond one person's comprehension. If you didn't feel alienated, you'd really be brainsick. You can't take any of this personally.

(HE *drinks from the bottle.*)

SHE: You should meditate. See the counselor. Make some I R L friends.

HE: I'm not a goldfish. I'm a goldfish's shadow.

SHE: I'll put in a good word for you at the Company during the Lady Tech Stars program. It's a fast track to management. A year tops. Then you can join me and I guess we'll connect the world or whatever. And you can ring the bell and we'll look back on this time and L O L. We'll tell dumb dad jokes on our breaks! Argh, it's driving me—

HE: I know you're lying. I know you reported me. (*He sets the empty wine bottle back into the bag.*)

SHE: I really didn't… Please. My mother needs me.

HE: You don't have a mother. You're a machine. And you've been L O L-ing at me this whole time.

SHE: Not at you. With you. Killing time to get through this insane job. It's just a job. If you don't like it, there's the door. That's what you'd tell me.

(HE *reaches into his bag.* SHE *backs away. He reveals his mobile device.*)

HE: You're right. Just a job. Let's shoot a selfie. Celebrate your big day. I never want to forget this special day for you. For us. You passed probation with the Contractor and became a Lady Tech Star at the Company on the same day. Must be a first. You're a pioneer. Get close. You like that angle? Does it please the lady?

SHE: Whatever.

(HE *wraps his arm around* SHE *and takes the picture.*)

HE: We can do better. (*He puts his cheek against hers.*) Smile. Come on. Anyone can smile on demand, right? Aww, come on. You're going to need this when you're at the Company. There. Oh. I think I see it. Bigger. With teeth. That's better. Good girl. That's great. We look cute. We could be a couple. A real human couple.

(SHE *tries to get away.* HE *grips her to him.*)

HE: We could get married. Have the one or two children allowed by our economic status. Maybe three kids since you're a Lady Tech Star, but wait no, that'd hurt your upward trajectory at the Company we can't have that. Wait, I know! We'll get a doggo to love!

SHE: You don't know what love is.

HE: Love is a loaded gun.

SHE: Stop saying that.

HE: Okay, you got me. I'm not actually in love with you, because how can I be? I'm the subject of a giant social engineering experiment run by technocratic elites who've hijacked the economy and are using us to build our own replacements. Maybe I only think I'm in love with you, like that AI who thinks it's human? Who knows? But I'm going to look you in the eyes and say I love you anyway, for the drama of it. You ready?

SHE: Please don't.

HE: I love you. Say it back. Please. Say it. Say it!!! *(He rings the bell and L O Ls.)* The look on your face! Ha ha ha. This is just another idea for my stage play. That they fall in love. The content moderators. I'm playing it out right now. Like improv. Ha ha ha.

SHE: I'm sure it'll be great.

HE: I'll tell you a secret. I finished it. I drafted it. It is done. I just need a title. I wanted to call it "The Goldfishes" but that's silly.

SHE: Call it "Moderation".

HE: I'm going to call it "Love is a Loaded Gun." But I need your permission to use that title. Do I have your permission?

SHE: Sure.

(The birds chirp.)

HE: I need a bio break.

SHE: Don't fall in.

(HE takes his bag and exits to the toilets, where he livestreams himself to the Platform and addresses the audience. SHE cowers at her desk and taps frantically at her mobile device.)

HE: Hey, everybody. So I'm uploading a draft of my manifesto to the TOR server. It's a screenplay that turns into a VR game that turns into a stageplay that turns into a manifesto about the way technology has turned us all into machine people and we haven't even noticed and most people don't care and humanity itself has pretty much been made into a global resource, a commodity, to serve hidden masters who in turn serve the big inhuman machine which is the un-sacred simulacrum of real life which doesn't exist anymore and maybe never did but we'd never know because our instincts are so eroded. I wrote this all down in a note.

Don't worry, there are some dick jokes too in my stage play manifesto so people can have a L O L. I was gonna call it "Love is Loaded Gun" but that's garbage so I'm gonna call it "Moderation." You'll get it when somebody stages the play. I hope you guys will remember me on this day, like Killdozer guy. You know? Remember me. That's all I want. It's "Moderation Day". Hashtag "moderation." Okay I'm going off script now. I'm uploading this good old fashioned note as well, for the record.

Please note: I didn't shoot up a mosque or a school or a synagogue or a sorority house or a Garlic festival or a country music show or a rap release or a Broadway show or a retail superstore or a cinema or a softball game or anything. I'm not a bad guy.

(HE *turns to her.* SHE *watches, listens. Moderates*)

HE: Please make copies of this video and my manifesto and spread it and save it locally so I don't disappear forever. *(He turns back to the audience.)* I know you guys will do that for me. Because the Company will remove this, almost immediately. Which is crazy because this is great content, right? I bet you think it's a joke. It's not another joke. I am not a joke. *(He pulls the gun from the bag.)* I am not a machine. And neither are you. And I'm not going to be brainsick anymore. I'm taking a bio break. So, guys and gal, thanks for tuning into my livestream. I hope you've enjoyed all the great content I've produced over the years! I hope you enjoyed all the dumb dad jokes! I'm going to go out with one of my favorites. Here we go! *(He puts the gun to his head.)*

So a pirate walks into a bar with a giant wheel on
his crotch. He squats into a stool on the bar and the
bartender looks at his parrot, then at the pirate's one
good eye. The bartender slaps a shot of rum onto the
bar and says, "Mr Pirate. You know there's a giant
wheel on your crotch?" To which the pirate replies—

(HE *is gone.* SHE *stands beside his desk in the light of the
moonlamp with her hand over the bell.*)

SHE: Argh. It's driving me nuts.
Remove. Suspend. Report.
Off with their heads.

END OF PLAY

www.ingramcontent.com/pod-product-compliance
Lightning Source LLC
Chambersburg PA
CBHW061640130726
47996CB00003B/1388